The Coolest Little Dinosaurs

AUTHOR & ILLUSTRATOR
MICHEL HARRIS

Copyright © 2020 by Aries Diamond Publishing. All rights reserved, no parts of this book may be used, or reproduced without the written permission of the author in any manner except for brief quotations embodied in critical articles, or reviews. Such requests can be inquired through Press Coordinator at: Writedreaminspire@gmail.com

Dedication

I dedicate this book to my sons who fill me with constant motivation & courage to live out my own dreams. You have made my life, so much better. Xai & Xani, you will always be mommy's coolest little dinosaurs.

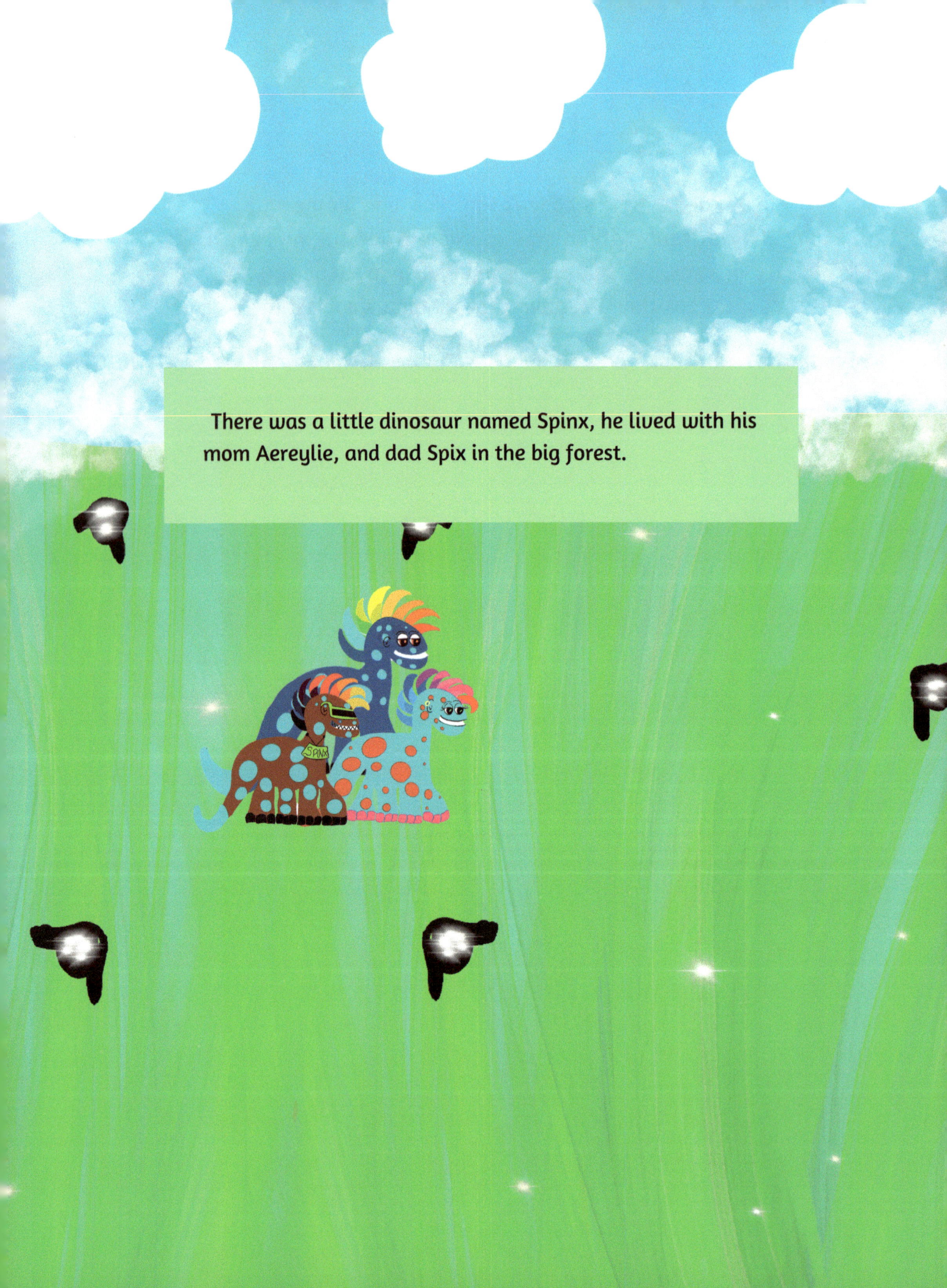

There was a little dinosaur named Spinx, he lived with his mom Aereylie, and dad Spix in the big forest.

Spinx loved the forest and all of his family adventures: he loved their Berry trees, going fishing, camping, and hiking. One of his favorite things to do was lay under the stars and hear stories his mom or dad would tell about their childhood when they were little dinosaurs.

As much as he enjoyed his families adventures, Spinx had big dreams of seeing the big city. He imagined what it might look like, and the cool adventures he could have there.

This made Spinx very sad, he was having a hard time understanding the world he lived in. How could a person judge you without ever knowing you?

A Stereo- what mom? What is that?

" A stereotype is an image or idea a person has about you based on what they think or believe. It can be based on how you look, race, ethnicity, or gender."

Well I think it is time to show the world who we are, and allow them to form their own opinions about dinosaurs. Let's show them we are different from the ideas they have about us. We don't mean them any harm, because we are really cool dinosaurs!

I can only hope they will accept us for who we are! I think it's time we all make a change, so let that change begin with us! I will be the change, I want to see in this world. What do you say?

Spinx

Spix can you believe we actually made it to the Big city?

Aereylie, I have wanted to experience this my whole life. Thank you Spinx for giving me the courage.

I am so excited. The buildings are so colorful and big. The food smells delicious. There are, so many adventures here.

As Spinx, Aereylie, and Spix walked through the city people were yelling, and screaming in fear!!! AAAAHH! DINOSAURS!! RUN FOR YOUR LIFE!!

Spinx and his family held their heads high while walking through the city, enjoying the scenery of the buildings, even with all of the commotion going on around them. They hoped that one day the people could see that Spinx and his family were not there to hurt them, but come to understand the dinosaurs were only there for an adventure, and would not cause them any trouble.

"I think we should run now"

"Hey Dude look, Cool Dinosaurs"

OMG

"STOP, DON'T GO THAT WAY!"

WHAT IN THE WORLD?

MAIL

SPINX

The city was breathtaking Spinx was happy for this experience it was even better than he had imagined. He and his parents were amazed at the cars riding by beeping their horns. Aereylie enjoyed the tall colorful buildings and delicious smells in the big city. Spix loved the sound of the hustle and bustle and all the interesting sites he took in.

Spinx was enjoying it all, especially the cool carnival nearby. He could hear the sounds of music radiating through the city. He saw lights flashing, and people laughing. Spinx imagined all the fun people were having and wished he was a part of it too. He would show off all his cool dance moves and the crowd would go crazy!

Spinx imagined the crowd cheering, and whispering at how Cool he and his family was. How cool it was to see dinosaurs in real life. Spinx could only wish for this day!!

DINOSAURS ARE SO COOL!!

DINOSAURS RULE!!

That night as Spinx, and his family laid under the stars they talked about their first adventure into the Big city. They would forever cherish the memories that was made that day. Spix found the courage to follow a lifelong dream. Aereylie was overjoyed to see her husband, and son accomplish their goals, and Spinx was finally able to see the world for himself. Spinx and his family were ready to embrace the world no matter how different, or scary it may seem. They were ready to accept people for who they were, and Hoped the world was ready to embrace them back. They would always be known as: The Coolest Little Dinosaurs!

www.ingramcontent.com/pod-product-compliance
Lightning Source LLC
Chambersburg PA
CBHW040419130526

44592CB00052B/2936